In The Small of My Backyard

In The Small of My Backyard

Matt Cook

Manic D Press
San Francisco

For Steve Cantin

Thanks to those who gave education and inspiration: Root, Cantin, Conant, Dewhurst, Firer, Haferman, Hazard, Holman, Kloss, Knox, McNally, McDaniel, my family, Penkalski, Robbins, Thacker, Wayland, and Wronski.

The author wishes to acknowledge the following publications and anthologies in which some of these poems originally appeared: *The Cream City Review*; *The United States of Poetry* (Abrams); *Revival: Spoken Word from Lollapalooza*; (Manic D Press); *Aloud: Voices from the Nuyorican Poets Café* (Henry Holt).

Published with the generous assistance of the California Arts Council.

Cover design: Scott Idleman/Blink

Library of Congress Cataloging-in-Publication Data

Cook, Matt, 1969–
  In the small of my backyard / Matt Cook.
    p. cm.
Poems.
  ISBN 0-916397-78-5 (alk. paper)
  1. Milwaukee (Wis.)--Poetry. 2. Working class--Poetry. I. Title.
PS3603.O6823 I5 2002
811'.6--dc21
                                2002003476

Contents

ONE

Around When I Was Born

There was a factory in my hometown that was called Rockford Screw—
It was something like the largest manufacturer of screws in the world.

Of course people had always made fun of that name;
People weren't born yesterday—
But there was a time and a place for that joke,
A more compartmentalized sense of civic maturity.

The mockery was a quiet mockery, one that was made sparingly,
One that coexisted with the basic practicality of lockwasher screws.

But sometime around when I was born
Some threshold of embarrassment had been crossed,
And Rockford Screw changed its name to
Rockford Cold Formed Products.

Holiday Promotional Gimmick

Every year around Christmastime,
A shopping mall in my hometown
Would have this holiday promotional gimmick
Where a guy dressed as Santa Claus
Would parachute into the shopping mall parking lot—
This would just happen every year.

One year, though, the parachute failed.
The costumed man falling from above—
The Santa Claus guy hitting the ground all dead.

It was true that he landed all dead
In my childhood doctor's backyard.
It was a Saturday afternoon in December—
My doctor was inside watching football on television.

Eventually, my doctor walked out to the garage
To get another log from the woodpile;
He saw a dead man dressed as Santa Claus in his backyard.

That Kid and His Mom

There was a kid on my block in the summertime
Who would punctuate a good joke by stepping on an ant—
I had a dream about the houses on that street,
A dream that looked like a kaleidoscope of old kitchen floors.

When he moved away to a farm, he had this lamb he named Bubbles.
Then one day the family sat down and ate Bubbles—
It was weird, he said, to eat something
That you were on a first name basis with.
Weird the way a beautiful funeral home was weird.

His mother came down with adult onset Christianity;
She would throw a lobster into a pot of boiling water
And then suddenly feel terrible, and try to save it—
As if that's what a Christian would do.

She wondered what it sounded like
When God talked babytalk to Jesus.

If a telephone pole fell in the street
And no one was there to hear it,
Would you call the phone company?

The Way I Tie My Shoes

When the Vietnam War ended
I didn't know how to tie my shoes.

But then the men started coming home from that war,
And they began to date my mother,
And then they were moving into our apartment,
And then they taught me how to tie my shoes.

This isn't some metaphor: as a boy I associated Vietnam War veterans
With people who knew how to tie their shoes.

This guy Murphy lived with us for a while.
He also taught me how to treat a snakebite
But that doesn't come up as often.

My uncle was over there—
He told me once that the jungle did strange things to his mind.
Then, while he was telling me this, he added, seemingly out of nowhere,
That he never liked deviled eggs as a child.
I couldn't see where he was going with that,
But then he laid this on me—
The jungle, for some reason, he said, caused him to crave deviled eggs.

That was it. That was his Vietnam story:
He developed a craving for deviled eggs.

My father, who was lucky at everything all the time,
Was stationed in Germany during the war.
All he did was play ping-pong and smoke marijuana and read paperbacks.
When he would go out on sentry duty,
He would carry just one bullet with him.
When his shift was over, he would hand the bullet
To the next man coming on.

Sometimes I'll sit transfixed in a chair, with one shoe on—
I'm working up the courage to put the next shoe on.
It's early in the morning, and the shoes look like big question marks.

Garage Sale

My great uncle escaped from the old folks home he was put in.
He walked right out the front door; he was not wearing any shoes.

He left with an acrylic landscape painting
He had stolen from the recreational room—
He walked to a nearby garage sale
Where, somebody said, he tried to sell the picture.

When he was found by the authorities later that night,
He was wearing a fedora for some reason.

I had a dream once about units of measurement
In which the actual reference standards had bodies with smiley faces.
The Imperial gallon was wearing a crown—
The U.S. gallon was wearing a fedora.

At my great uncle's funeral,
There was a strong wind
That blew my hat into his grave.
I was happy it worked out that way.

Drunk Guy

I am a direct descendant of someone
Who fell off a bar stool
And broke his collarbone.

The men at the bar, he said,
Gave him drunken medical advice.

Someone suggested he lay
Perfectly flat against the floor
And roll over, back and forth,
As evenly as he could.

Friends tried to make
Slings out of bar towels;
People composed
Narratives to tell his wife.

I know that when a lobster wants to climb out of a cage,
The other lobsters will hold on to him,
And pull him back down into the cage.

I saw him another time on Halloween;
His face was all bloodied.
I honestly did not know
If it was a costume.

Galoshes

He said that life was like taking out the garbage;
He said that death was like looking at your house from across the street.

He had this idea regarding equestrian statues—
He said that in the future,
Instead of having a statue of a general or somebody on a horse,
They would have statues of really important people driving their cars.

He avoided pizza until some young people told him to eat it—
He's driving back from the pizzeria, he's walking through the door,
He's holding the pizzas sidelong under his arm
As though they were books from the library.

He visited New York City in the wintertime,
He went around to stores looking to buy galoshes—
But he found that the people who worked
In the sort of places that would carry galoshes
Were new to the English language; and galoshes, he found out,
Were among the last English words that people learn.

He tried calling them waterproof overshoes,
But by the time anyone understood him, it was spring outside.
My grandfather is dead now.

My grandmother is still walking around,
She lives down in Illinois,
Belongs to a quilting club there.
I asked her recently if there was a big problem these days
With people sharing needles in sewing circles.
She's smart enough to laugh at something like that.

Between Shitty and Ideal

Father actually broke his thumb once pulling on a pair of socks.
They were *argyle* socks, I think, that broke his thumb—

Our world has room for socks that involve knitting schemes
Of overlapping diamond-shaped areas—
The freedom to define oneself somehow through socks—
That's *so interesting*, when you think of it.

Father gets out of the shower, or something.
His feet are still wet, or something.
He's in a hurry; he's *struggling* to pull these socks on—
His hand slips or whatever,
It slams back against the woodwork of this sofa, or whatever.

He breaks his thumb that way—just like that,
With feelings of *unmingled stupidity*.
Coming home from the hospital,
His thumb swathed in a light gauze dressing.

I have a memory of him talking to his brother
About this over the telephone:
I remember him saying that the situation was *far from ideal*—

Those were his words: "This is far from ideal."
But he added that it wasn't exactly *shitty* either.

Father described the situation as falling somewhere between shitty and ideal.

Someone to Love Me

We had this snake that lived in a glass box in our front room—
This was somewhere during childhood.

The snake had broken its promise to amuse us;
We had broken our promise to find him amusing.

He became a conversation piece for tossed-out love;
People would notice him, and then they would feel bad.

Like going over to somebody's house; they have a stationary bicycle—
Immediately it suggests a failed exercise regiment.

We go anyway down to the pet shop,
Where they sell laboratory rodents in Chinese carryout boxes.

Of course the rodents were engineered to die,
But because pretty fish were sold in the same boxes,
There were words along the side of the box that read:
I've finally found a home—I've finally found someone to love me.
An illustration was there too—
Some image that referenced togetherness,
Something involving hands—I forget.

My father would always say the same thing—
He would say this, and only this, to the pet store guy:
Give me the worst mouse you've got.

Privilege

I was living in the basement
Of my father's Georgian Colonial mansion—
This was back during college somewhere.

I had all these *psychological* problems—
But I was all *privileged* and shit,
So I just went to doctors, and went to *college* all day.

At night, my father and I would sit around in his office
Watching videotapes of BBC Shakespeare productions.

Once, when we were doing that, the phone rang.
With the remote control,
Dad shut off the video,
Causing the regular TV to come on.

On the screen there was an advertisement
For a hungry child in a developing country with
Bugs flying around his food—
Dad's phone conversation was *hurried*, and to the point.

Upholstered Chairs

My father had these two huge dogs
That looked more like upholstered chairs than dogs.
This was back when I was living in the basement
Of my father's Georgian Colonial mansion—

I had all these psychological problems—
But it gave me a certain tattered respectability
To walk my father's dogs for money.
He had these two huge dogs
That looked more like upholstered chairs than dogs.

Dad would come home from work,
And a scene like this might play out:

He would pay me the dog-walking money,
Then I would try to gamble it against him on this pool table we had.
I wanted to make more money, so that I could buy drinks at a bar.

But Dad was a better pool player, so he would end up winning—
He would just win all his money back.

But then he would feel sorry for me,
He would end up giving me all the money back anyway—
Then he would ask me if I needed a ride to the bars.

Disposable Pens

I get money in the mail from my grandmother—
She's *my* National Endowment for the Arts.
A check at the end of the month—
It's our victory in the Second World War,
It's still reaching me somehow.

The *penmanship* is still connected to the nineteenth century.
Penmanship—the word itself is formidable,
Suggests a certain minimal standard.
To even describe my younger brother's handwriting as 'penmanship'
Gives way to a comical sense of exaggerated formality.

I found this dead art deco fountain pen
Down by a drain in the basement of a house I was painting.
The fountain pen was a semi-precious object—
But America had had it up to here with precious objects;
Such objects required *maintenance*.

That's the beauty of disposable artifacts—
You don't have to *worry* about their maintenance;
You don't have to concern yourself with their fate.

Of course, I am an authentic American poet—
I *always* write with disposable pens.

But whenever I have *something to say*,
And the presence of mind to write that something down,
I can never find my pen—

I suppose that's what we *get*,
For using disposable pens.

Banking

I had this great uncle who was like really into *banking*—
He was like a *banker*, or something.
But the thing was, he was like really shitty at it—
He wasn't any good at it;
His bank would keep *failing* all the time.

So whenever this would happen,
He would just start some other bank with some other guy—
He could always find some other guy;
But then they would open up this bank, and *it* would fail.

He would just keep *moving* his family around to different places,
Trying to find some place where his *banks* wouldn't fail,
But they just *continued* to fail.
He kept blaming shit on regional circumstances, like *droughts* or whatever.

This was back when people would just go into banking by like *buying a safe*
And then just *putting it in a room*, and then just putting up a sign outside—
Just *calling* yourself a banker.

I can remember even *my mom* telling me that her uncle wasn't that *bright*—
My mom said he was just all *diligent*.

The Parking Lot Didn't Help

His mother threatened to make oatmeal for his father,
But his father had already made oatmeal for himself.
Modern medicine is such a miracle;
Especially that part about the waste washing up along the beach.

There was a greater sense of potato chips out West:
They turned a corner, and his mom tried to explain the family.
The parking lot didn't help much;
He thought of something funny to say about his dad.

His mother said he was comparing apples and oranges.
His mother never understood
That apples and oranges were the only things worth comparing;
That poets were put here by something or someone
To give people insights into apples and oranges.

His mother was never close to *her* father,
She filed a lawsuit against him over petty charges,
So that they could be together in court.

A Box of Chocolates

He grew up on a hardscrabble cul-de-sac.
The father who would abuse him with tennis balls.
The social worker who would find
Bruises consistent with tennis balls—

The newspapers became yellow
Exactly the way the guacamole became brown—
Drama has a way of sitting around for a while and becoming melodrama.
Then it sits around some more and becomes
Monkeys throwing custard pies.
It's the failure, of course, that makes it funny;
Watching drama *fail* is funny.

The father on television had to walk the mother over to the ocean—
A person on television just does this, whenever there is
Something terrible to say.
You place the mother within a *life goes on* context.

Sometimes, the comedy breaks down in the body, and
Becomes a carbohydrate.
More often, it becomes less and less funny—
It becomes something akin to *social studies*.

Time always works *against* author's intent.
It always works toward *failure*.
If a man tells you that Shakespeare is *timeless*,
Do not take that man seriously.
Shakespeare is something Americans give out like a box of chocolates.

When his parents got divorced,
Jesus Christ could still visit God on the weekends.

If you're not part of the comedy, you're part of the tragedy.

Bladders in the Windpipe

My descendants came over on some very early boats.
They were generic Colonial American aristocrat people.

This was back when aristocrats would fashion their own dresses
Using leftover silk from old socks.
That's what aristocrats did back then—
They made their own dresses out of *socks*.

The Revolution was going on,
But armies were so *polite* back then.
They stopped fighting one another in the wintertime.
They wouldn't go on marches when it was cold and slippery outside.

My Great Something Grandfather was a lawyer—
He was always getting people out of *jams*.
This was back when courtrooms had fireplaces in them—
The bailiff or somebody would go over and stir up the logs.

My Great Something Grandmother had babies
That died of things like *bladders in the windpipe*.
When I read about that, it sounded so antiquated to me.
I immediately asked this hospital guy I knew
What exactly that was, and what they would call a condition like that now.
He said that they *still* call it bladders in the windpipe.

TWO

To Capitalize Ungodly

In Colonial America
People would fire up the oxcart,
Go into town, and trade hay for firewood.
Then they would come home from all that, and unload the firewood.
Then they would sit around and read Virgil.

Men who could stack firewood neatly
Were considered good marriage prospects—
People would give out slaves as wedding presents.

During the wintertime, shopkeepers would scatter oyster shells
On sidewalks to improve footing.
People wondered whether or not to capitalize 'ungodly'.

For fun, people would have simple boating parties.
People would get malaria and then their ears would start ringing.

Remember that painting, that Gilbert Stuart painting of Washington?
Sure you remember that thing, everybody does, the really famous one—
Seriously, I used to like that picture a lot,
But then I realized that everything Stuart ever did looked like Washington.
I saw this self-portrait Stuart made of himself—
It looked exactly like Washington.

Books Out to Yale

That Calvinist guy, Jonathon Edwards—
Everybody thought he was so *impressive*
Because he went to Yale when he was only twelve;
But it's really not that impressive, because when Edwards was twelve,
Yale was only four.

Yale had something like three buildings at that time—
That was it for buildings at Yale back then.
They had like one farmhouse where all the freshmen lived;
One farmhouse.

They had seven shelves of books—
That was Yale's library;
That's how many books Yale had.

But then this wealthy philanthropy guy named Dummer—
That was actually his name, *Dummer*, Jeremiah Dummer—
Decided he would give all his books to Yale.

Dummer had this really comprehensive private library,
But it was more or less just vanity.
He never actually read anything.

But when he was old
Nobody was impressed with his books anymore—
Philanthropy was the only way he could still draw attention to himself—
So he decided he would give all his books to Yale.

The donation was called The Dummer Gift—that's what he wanted it called.
He packed the books up in wooden crates and loaded them onto oxcarts,
And then he wheeled them out toward Yale.

But along the road, a group of bad people came along,
And pushed over the oxcarts, and stole The Dummer Gift.

One of the bad people also threw a sharp, heavy rock at Dummer.
The rock struck Dummer about the head and hurt him badly.

Apart from like *always wear a helmet*, or something,
There really isn't a whole lot, like in the way of a moral or something,
That you can really draw from something like that.

President Garfield

He had this childhood fascination with ships and things like that—
He was just some kid in Ohio looking out at Lake Erie
And there'd be like ships going by, and he'd be like,
"Wow, I wish I could be on those ships."

There was this woods near his house,
And whenever a steam locomotive would go by
It would throw off sparks and the woods would catch on fire.
This would just keep happening every time a locomotive went by.
So his dad was trying to fight this forest fire one day,
And he just got all exhausted and
Caught a cold and died. People would just catch a cold and
Die in those days.

So his mom is all single mom trying to raise Garfield.
And they got this farm and shit,
And Garfield's got these brothers and
They're trying to work this farm.
But Garfield just sits around all day reading pirate books,
Then he just says to his mom,
I don't want to be a farmer, I want to be a carpenter instead—let's build a house.
So he gets these carpenters together and they build a house, and
When the house is all done he's like,
 I'm still obsessed with pirates; I want to go sailing.

So he goes to Cleveland and tries to get on a boat there,
But the captains in Cleveland
Just end up treating him disdainfully; so Garfield's all pissed,
But he's too proud to go home,
So he just takes the first job that comes along that has
Anything to do with watercraft.
He's working on this barge that carries horses and coal—
Just going up and down canals all day with horses and coal.
But it turns out, after all of this, that Garfield is actually a really shitty sailor;

He keeps falling into the water and catching fevers and shit,
And so finally he's like, *Fuck this, I'll become a teacher.*

He worked his way through college by ringing bells;
People who needed their bells rung,
Like churches and crap would pay him money to ring
Their bells; I'm serious.
In no time he's a professor of ancient languages, just right after
Dealing with horses and coal.
He would actually show off for chicks by writing Greek with one hand,
While at the same time writing Latin with the other.
He would show his appreciation for a pun by *groaning.*

Anyway, after about a year he's like,
Wait a second—slavery's a drag; I'll go into politics.
Then he became a state representative;
Then he became a U.S. representative;
Then he became a senator; then he became a president;
Then he was shot.

When Garfield was shot, doctors were trying to deal with this bullet
That was lodged in his vertebrae and shit.
But they couldn't handle the situation; it was
Somehow too complicated or something.
So they brought in Alexander Graham Bell
Because he was the fanciest scientist we had walking around.
So Bell tried to remove the bullet with this electrical device.
He brought along his electrical device to take care of the situation.
But it didn't work out; the bullet remained all lodged in
Garfield's vertebrae. So he just died; The End.

All His Rubber Away

They had spies in Honolulu with fishing poles testing for torpedo depth.
If they think, that we think, that they think, that we think it's Pearl;
Then it's probably the Philippines.
It was Pearl.
But then again, when they saw Babe Ruth blow a bubble,
They thought he was blowing his stomach inside out.

Coney Island whitefish were found as far off as New Guinea—
They rode torpedoes to get there.
Referring to something easily accomplished as a *cakewalk*,
Was the only American colloquialism
The headshrinkers of New Guinea bothered to learn.
The average Japanese man
Learned the twenty most important verbs and gave up.
Generals knew more—
Tojo dared Yamamoto to call up Rita Hayworth
And say, Yank My Doodle, It's a Dandy.

Always fly your plane upside-down;
It's harder for someone to read your serial number.

Big city pilots like Butch O'Hare
Didn't mind crashing in shark-infested waters:
It was a lot like walking through a really bad neighborhood.
When Butch O'Hare died on St. Patrick's Day,
The entire Army wore green.

Meanwhile, back at the ranch,
Eleanor Roosevelt was in charge—
FDR was always out playing wheelchair basketball—
Until he got transferred from sickbay to a rubber room.

And then they had to take all his rubber away for the war effort.

Washington D.C.

First visit there—
I get off the train,
I walk into a men's room.

The first words I hear,
In our nation's capital,
A man says: "I'll suck your dick for two dollars."

I just ignore him—
Because I only have big bills on me.

I don't know what I expected—
Maybe I expected the Second Coming
Of the Father of Our Country
With polyester teeth
And wooden pants.

Elvis Island

The currency of his native country was worthless here—
His paper money was good for nothing except
Making Oriental rugs for somebody's doll house.

One of the first things he noticed about America
Was that his lies were no longer powerful;
Nobody understood what he was talking about;
Nobody spoke his language.

He had to learn the language
From girls down at the shopping mall.
But they spoke entirely in similes—
Everything was—
Like, I don't know.

People will smuggle themselves across borders in refrigerated trucks,
And then their grandchildren will want to go to film school.

THREE

Mom in Milwaukee

My mother doesn't understand why we live in Milwaukee.
Every time she visits, it's always the grayest, ugliest day outside.

People who look like deformed potatoes are urinating in public;
Disturbed war veterans are combing the lawns of the county park system
With those metal detector things.

Motorists at stoplights next to you
Are altogether unapologetic
About littering Chicken McNugget dipping sauce containers
Out passenger-side windows.

You'll see a car for sale in a vacant lot—
A tree growing through its engine.
You'll see the ruins of a dead snowman, or something.

Then Mother leaves town—
At once the sunbeams break through the clouds,
Passersby look beautiful and sophisticated.
Garbage men have top hats and cigarette cases—
The ranch houses have simian gargoyles.
Independent rock and roll bands are tolerably harmonious
And the Mexican food is suddenly better than *New* Mexico.

Suckers

A girl at a Milwaukee bar
Was not drinking.
She unwrapped a sucker
And put it in her mouth.

A drunk man,
Thinking the sucker was a cigarette,
Reached over with a match to light it.

The girl,
Taking the sucker out of her mouth,
Said to the drunk,
"It's not a cigarette, it's, uh, lollypop."

She only said 'lollypop' because
She did not want to say 'sucker'
To the drunk who wanted to light her cigarette.

A baby boom is when
Two suckers are born every minute.

Integrity

I was baptized at a bus stop in Milwaukee
By a mad woman who squirted contact lens solution at me.
I knew immediately that it was a baptism—because she told me it was.
She said flatly that I had *received* the Holy Spirit.
I was baptized at a bus stop with contact lens solution.

If solitary confinement were outlawed
Only outlaws would have solitary confinement.

Guns don't caulk windows; people caulk windows.
I like having integrity; it's cheap entertainment.

If something audible only to a dog falls in a forest,
And no dog is there to hear it,
Can we just call that a mystery?

Corresponding Idiots

I saw a man in a Milwaukee bar,
Reading the obituaries in a Chicago paper.

That guy really knew how to enjoy himself.

This was a dumpy Milwaukee bar called The Schmidt House.
A hand-painted sign over the door,
Sign says, 'Schmidt House'
Alongside a crude drawing of an outhouse.
I thought about the owner of the place—
Imagine your livelihood is a business whose name is a pun on shit.

I thought about Johnny Cash and Fats Domino.
Men whose names gave rise to the corresponding idiots
Johnny Paycheck and Chubby Checker—
To have one's name legally changed
To something that would forever cast you as second rate.

The Rite of Spring

At a Milwaukee bus stop
I overheard one guy explaining to another guy
That his girlfriend wasn't really pregnant,
That she just had this tumor that gave her the appearance of
Being pregnant.

People rioted
When Stravinsky put on *The Rite of Spring*
But it wasn't because the music was somehow beyond them,
It was because people had went without sausages and shoelaces
For two months so that they could be transported from drudgery,
And Stravinsky let them down.

Yet whenever dudes break into your car
It's always the same sort of patterns: window or door broken;
Contents of glove-compartment thrown onto passenger seat;
Never any attention paid to challenging the conventions of robbery—
When dudes break into your car,
They tend to be very traditional.

Yet I waited tables at this 24-hour pancake house graveyard shift:
This sex worker sits down at the counter,
Orders a glass of buttermilk.
I bring her a glass of buttermilk,
She says, "This is sour, bring me a new glass."
I bring her a new glass
She says, "This is sour, bring me a new glass."
I bring her another glass of buttermilk
She says, "This is sour, bring me a new glass."

Meanwhile there's a washed-up musicologist sitting next to her,
A rockabilly scholar wearing retrogressive pantaloons.

The rockabilly scholar says this to the sex worker: "Lady,
If you don't know what buttermilk tastes like, you got problems."

Where They Were and What They Were Doing

I was looking through Milwaukee newspapers
From the day after John F. Kennedy was shot—

There was this auto body worker
Who brought his BB gun to work that day;
He was arrested for shooting his BB gun
Out the windows of the body plant
At passing automobiles—

That's where he was and what he was doing
On the day President Kennedy was assassinated.

Then there was this *biochemist*.
He was giving this speech at some university in town—
He was *inviting* the audience to imagine
A strain of pneumonia bacteria
That was wearing *a heavy armor suit* that was actually made of *protein*—
That was his public speaking metaphor.
His *point* was that the protein would act like
A shield against white blood cells.
That's what *that guy* was up to that day.

And just outside of town somewhere,
A car slammed into a truck on a rainy highway.
The car guy *died* of head injuries;
The truck guy was in *satisfactory condition* with neck pain.

In satisfactory condition with neck pain—
That's where that guy was, and what he was doing.

The day President Kennedy was shot,
These kids broke into a junior high school.
They stole twenty dollars worth of stamps,
And smashed up an aquarium.

That was their story;
That's where they were and what they were doing.

Avocado Toilets

We saw this avocado-colored toilet in the street one day
It was one of those days
       when people were putting things in the street
We came up with this idea to put this avocado-colored toilet
In the back of this guy we didn't like's truck
So we went and found this guy's truck
And we put this avocado-colored toilet
Right in the back of this guy's truck
Had a good laugh about it
Forgot about it
A year goes by   we're driving around again
We see another avocado-colored toilet
Just like before   virtually identical
So we go and find that guy's truck again
And we put this avocado-colored toilet
Right in the back of his truck again
We just kept putting things in his truck
We thought it would send him on an emotional rollercoaster
But it didn't work
He was too well-adjusted
It didn't phase him
He thought they were just green toilets
That's why he was a guy we didn't like

Even as a Boy

I wrote smart, beautiful poetry
That was taken away by an elementary school teacher.

Some student was making *a lovely presentation*,
But I was recording ideas in my notebook,
Which was at odds with elementary education.

I was writing a poem
About a man with food in his beard.

Nobody ever took my father's notebooks away,
Because my father slept with his notebooks—
Exactly the way responsible fathers should.

Nevertheless, the taco restaurant closed temporarily
Because they decided to lay new carpeting down with fancy glue.
And there were no girls anywhere.

Somewhere in there, a waiter brought complimentary coffee to my father.
But the coffee was terrible; so my father complained.
This was justifiable; complimentary beverages are often terrible.
Usually, they are terrible.

The teacher would always kill class time by handing back old papers,
Which made sense to me, even as a boy.

Broken Intellectuals

I had this adolescent fascination with *broken intellectuals*—
Old men who hung around at university student unions.
The relationship was like a transaction; I would buy them coffee,
And they would tell me something in the way of *old wise man shit.*

Of course I knew they were broken failures; that wasn't the point.
When they would tell some story, I wouldn't even follow the narrative—
I would only pay attention to the *soaring voices.*

They were like poetry vending machines;
You would put small change into them,
And literature would sometimes fall out.

I know that in London they have a problem with *insufferable bibliophiles*
Who loiter around and get thrown out of bookstores for talking too much.
They are treated exactly the way homeless men in America
Are treated in 24-hour pancake restaurants—

Nobody liked the broken intellectuals as much as I did—
Other boys would actually become *outraged*
When they would loan money to broken intellectual storytellers,
Only to never be paid back.

Those boys were so *deprived* of a poetical sense—
Who did they think they were?
Their parents must not have warned them—
Never loan money to a storyteller.

Art History

This *broken intellectual* once told me
That when Cezanne painted the poker players,
The picture was so convincing
That you could look at it
And you could tell who was winning the card game.

Van Gogh's potato eaters, he said,
That was another matter—
You could look at *that thing*
And you could tell they were eating potatoes.

James Joyce

James Joyce
He was stupid
He didn't know as much as me
I'd rather throw dead batteries at cows
Than read him
Everything was going fine
Before he came along
He started the Civil War
He tried to get the French involved
But they wouldn't listen
They filled him up with desserts
He talked about all the great boxers
That came from Ireland,
Like he trained 'em or something
Then he started reading some of his stuff
Right as we told him to get lost
He brought up the potato famine
We said, "Your potatoes are plenty good.
Deal with it! Work it out somehow!"
Then he said, "America must adopt the metric system.
It's much more logical." We said, "No!
We like our rulers! Go away!"
Thomas Jefferson said,
"You always get the rulers you deserve."

Madagascar

It was proposed
That troughs of tasty gruel be erected
Along Wisconsin Avenue
So that weary shoppers could refresh themselves—
But somebody had to stand up and say, *define gruel*.

My grandfather always said,
Semantics can take a bath in my ass, and probably would.

The people who should swing from trees never do.
The Spanish Armada got blown into matchsticks
Long before they ever got a chance
To sell oranges along 14th street.

Leonardo could have easily invented the bicycle,
But he had to jump straight to the helicopter instead;
The best people I know are always jumping straight to the helicopter.

My grandfather always said,
There'll be octopi in the sky when you die.

There was an octopus on every street corner when I was born.
Sometimes an octopus is just an octopus.
America is a nation where you cannot bum a cigar—
I bought some cigars,
I gave them away,
South of the border down Mexico way.

You put the bombs in old Bombay.
You put the cows in old Moscow.
You put the kooks in Cucamonga.
You put Gordo in Alamagordo
You put the gas in my car in Madagascar
And you wouldn't even know where that was if you didn't play Risk.

Some kids didn't play Risk.
They had to learn about Madagascar in the locker rooms
And on the playgrounds.
Misconceptions abounded.

Science Was Invented By A Bunch of Guys Who Were So Ugly They Couldn't Possibly Believe In God

How smart are we?
We descended from apes
Now we dress like them on Halloween

It is said that a barrel of monkeys are fun
Monkeys evolved into humans who invented barrels to put monkeys in
So it would be fun
Monkeys aren't any fun on their own
So maybe it's just barrels that are fun

Shooting fish in a barrel is supposed to be easy
This makes simple Darwinian sense
Barrels were fashioned by natural selection to make shooting fish easy
Monkey see monkey do was the first example of eye-hand coordination
The pie in the face was next
I threw a birthday cake at The Man Who Shot Liberty Valance
He was 24

Nowadays we can't figure out why smallpox is so funny

Tyrannosaurus Rex didn't really look like that
He wasn't really built like that
Walking upright
          on two legs with those dinky little arms
          eating flesh like that
There's no way he could hunt like that
He was a veggo if ever there was one

We found a bunch of bones lying around
And we think we know how they fit together
Right
They've arranged those bones all sorts of ways
They've come up with all sorts of crazy-shaped beasts

This one just happens to look the most ferocious
Some kid probably liked it the best
It sells dinosaur books

Intellectual Property

We noticed ourselves and acted accordingly,
Which was a singular innovation among living things.

Apes were the only animals
That really understood how to ape anything.

A hedgehog could not ape something;
It could only hedgehog something—
Which brought about no progress.

The Stone Age began
When somebody saw somebody throw a rock at somebody,
And stones became our friends suddenly.

The written word allowed apes that weren't apes anymore
To store ideas;
So that books could become Tupperware for nonsense.

But the storage of wordplay
Gave way to the notion that notions could be bought and sold.
Intellectual property made aping against the law—
Evolution became plagiarism.

People stopped going outside to learn things from the streets and sidewalks;
They stayed inside and aped frauds of reality they had seen on television—
They made counterfeits of counterfeits;
Like a violin player practicing mistakes.

Then my little brother gets stopped by the police;
He swears they interrogated him
Exactly as they had seen actors playing cops on TV
Interrogate actors playing suspects on TV.

The way my cat thinks it's somehow my fault
When the weather gets hot in the summertime—

I wonder whether these things were even considered
Back when God edited the universe.

Somehow Preferable

Working janitorial at the university,
The voice of my boss comes over the walkie-talkie—
Somebody vomited on the center staircase;
Could I please go take care of that, please.

I imagine the creamy stomach acids of a mediocre business student.

But I make my way to the staircase,
And I see instead a little boy—
He's just waiting there; he's standing guard over his responsibility;
He's looking to pass it on to someone else.

I feel better right away—
A shift away from workplace dread,
A misplaced sense of community service.
I find something decent and honorable
About mopping up little boy vomit.

The way a ladybug landing in your soup
Is somehow preferable to a fly.

Other People's Money

Of course poetry is something you discover
Through a process of daydreaming and talking to yourself.

I'm still searching the want ads—
Growing company seeks distant skeptic
With messy hair, who asks a lot of questions.

I recommend janitorial work at a university,
Where they will leave you alone in the shadows
To tie up garbage bags like calves at a rodeo.

That was always my job
Until the poetry I discovered there,
Through daydreaming and talking to myself,
Allowed me to get teaching positions.

Other people's money was something you would find
Underneath cooling units when everybody went home.

I would imagine another time,
A time when my great grandmother
Might have bought a pair of shoes
With that dollar seventy-five.

There must have been a more sincere joy—
A sort of exalted rapture about finding money in the street.

And those who dropped money in the street
Must have had a different vocabulary—
They probably said things like,
I seem to have misplaced fifteen cents.

FOUR

The Motorman's Friend

He was still trying to win an argument
He had had with a girl four years ago;
Still running through the rhetorical combinations,
Imagining the perfect comeback.

He drove a bus for the county—
He wore a specialized rubber pouch
To empty his bladder into.
You would call something like that
The motorman's friend, he said.

He took modern psychotropic drugs,
Which essentially gave him the false confidence of beer,
But he could still operate heavy machinery.

He was tired of always hearing on television
That breakfast was the most important meal of the day.

He actually made a point of eating
Breakfast everyday for six months—
I think he was fully expecting that this would transform him
Into a doctor or a lawyer or something.

But after all those breakfasts
He was still the same person,
So he just stopped eating breakfast.

We still talk sometimes on the phone.

Roofing

He worked as a roofer, but the job drove him mad
Because he was always looking down on people
Who were looking down *on him* because he was a roofer—
He spent his days at a forty-five degree angle
Looking down on people who were looking down on him.

He couldn't tell his dreams from his nights at the bar
From his phone conversations with the phone company.

His dreams were about men who fed fish with smaller fish,
In wagons that recalled the western frontier,
With Asian elephants doing all sorts of mystifying shit—
The bigger the animal was, the bigger its mythology was.
The older his dad got, the bigger his TV got.

Your Entertainment Dollar

We paid money to sit in the dark
And watch people pretend to cry;
To watch people pretend to die;
To watch Greeks pretend to be Indians.

We bought a dozen eggs,
And nine of them were broken—
We went out for coffee afterwards,
We discussed ways in which the broken ones
Could have been better, could have been more convincing.

Really Bad Letters

Never write poetry about sex because
When it's bad it's terrible
And when it's good
It's still pretty bad.

I tried to write poetry like that once
Because a girl asked me to,
But the result was lousy and unreadable.

The only line worth saving
Was an obscure reference to a newspaper headline
Regarding an investigation by zoo workers—
Something about a month-long probe into alleged elephant abuse.

This was a girl who truly believed
That the Scrabble brand crossword board game
Made excellent foreplay.

But she took the game a lot more seriously than did I
Which meant that she would swear and get mad
And exhale in exaggerated ways and so on
When play didn't go her way.

And she would only want to fuck me
When she was stuck with really bad letters.

The Problem with the Banana

I woke up one morning with a fruit company sticker on my ass.
Something like a Costa Rican banana label—
Just stuck to my ass one morning.

There was no satisfying explanation for any of this—
I never eat bananas; possibly, there has not been a banana
Anywhere near my bed for years.

Perhaps these things upset me more than they should;
Mysteries remind me that I don't know where dead souls go.

But my girlfriend was raised by MIT scientists
Who taught her to believe
That everything could be logically explained.

When I show her a poem,
She will say that there are fifty thousand atoms
That make up a period on a typed page—
Something about electrons whirling around a nucleus—
And in between the electrons and the nucleus, she says,
There is nothing—just dead space where nothing goes on.

Yet I could never even comprehend
The economics of how Marshall Field's
Stayed in business downtown,
And then they went out of business—
So they couldn't comprehend it either.

The whole problem with the banana was instantly knowable to her,
She just said this firmly:
"Obviously, there was a fruit sticker in our bed,
And it became affixed somehow to your ass."

She actually explained nothing;
The problem with the banana will never be knowable.

I Was Wrong

We're at this backyard party—
She's walking around with this video camera;
She's collecting all this *footage* of the backyard party.

Then she announces that everyone needs to go inside;
That everyone needs to watch this videotape of the party on TV,
Even though the actual party is *still going on* outside.

People agree to do this without even thinking, because she is pretty—
She says that she's an experimental filmmaker;
She says that she's a *good* experimental filmmaker—
I wonder if that's like being good at playing with your food.

But it turned out that I was wrong about everything—
I ended up *marrying* the experimental filmmaker.

He Had a Way

We had no place to stay except with these drug users,
Who had a shack on a piece of land with a chicken coop.

The chickens were ornamental;
Nobody ate them or took them to market or anything.
The land, apparently, was owned by some rich guy—
He had no problems with any of this.

One of the boys who lived there
Had a way of buying used mountain bicycles
And then gluing wood chips all over them.

That way, he could give the bicycles a vague, earthy quality;
He could take them into town, he could sell them for
More than he paid for them.
He had a way of making bicycles that looked as though
They were covered with oversized bacon bits.

He also refused to eat honey;
Something having to do, he said, with imprisoned honeybees.
It became a question of insect rights—
He had a way of embroiling you in a discussion of insect rights.

Mexican Insane Asylums

He'd come up with really good Twenty Questions guys
Like veteran character actor Simon Oakland—
The guy who came in at the end of *Psycho* and explained everything.

I damn near stumped his ass
On the nineteenth century chef Duncan Hines.
He's on question 19
He goes into the bathroom
Takes a piss
Washes his hands really good
Comes out and says, "Duncan Hines?"
He's in a really good mood for the rest of the day.

He gets me on that Mexican artist guy—Rodriguez?
I never even heard of the guy.
He was in a Mexican insane asylum around the turn of the century.
They never gave him all the art supplies he wanted
So he had to use masticated food—
Got me thinking what kind of food was served
At Mexican insane asylums around the turn of the century—
Turns out it was top notch.

We're in this trivia bowl team called
The Undersea World of Leon Klinghoffer.
He's got me into wearing black suits to all the competitions;
He's got this big theory about black suits,
Says that French existentialists wore black suits around—
I wish they did.
Turns out my dad's a French existentialist
And this poem is just a way for me to write myself out of that jam—
Turns out it works, and I'm happy as a clam when it's all done.

Kalamazoo

His parents were perfectly cool—
They would build fires with the financial section of the newspaper.

And yet he moved through life,
Getting very angry at poorly designed parking lots.

He went up to Alaska to work on salmon industry boats
Only to act surprised when the men he worked alongside
Proved to be really bad conversationalists.

Nevertheless, he said, if you had access to stupid bikini underwear,
Men on the Japanese boats would trade
Their Samurai swords for that stupid bikini underwear—
It wasn't until he got home that he realized
That Samurai swords were stupid, too.

Is sealskin even waterproof?
Of course it's waterproof;
Your own skin's waterproof—
When you take a shower does your heart get wet?
Jesus Christ.

There were Indians once who named a river Kalamazoo,
Because the water in the river was all bubbly;
And Kalamazoo, it turns out, means *bubbly water.*

Rugged Individualism

I had a nightmare about being
Trapped in an elevator with a self-made man—
He was born with a silver bootstrap in his mouth;
He pulled himself up by his spoons.

But when he lived in the fraternity,
Before he could roll his sleeves up and get anything done,
He would pack his laundry into boxes
And mail it off to his mother and his grandmother—
They would wash and iron his clothes,
And then mail them back to him.

Now when I talk to him over the phone,
It's like I'm an Indian,
And he's the government.

When he tells me that money is tight,
He sounds like a bulimic girl
Who wants to lose ten pounds.

I found an Emily Post etiquette book in his basement—
It was stolen from a library.

Carp Gallbladders

.

I was reading an academic medical journal once,
Just to see what that would feel like.

There was something in there
About this weird disease that was identified.
It kept showing up in Chinatowns across the country—
Nobody could figure out what the deal was with it.

Finally the disease was linked to *carp gallbladders*—
Residents in these sections were eating
Ridiculously authentic food that featured carp gallbladders.

Then some fraternity brothers at a major state university
Came down with the same sickness—
And nobody could think of any lifestyle parallel
Between middle-class frat boys and poor, urban Asians.

But then through a lot of trial and error and stuff
It was determined that the frat boys
Got the disease from drinking games
Like swallowing goldfish,
Which are a type of carp,
The End.

I've got a friend from Iceland;
He said this to me the other day:

"Americans are always telling you about some article they've read."

Ping Pong

When you need someone
To fix your hot water heater,
You have to page through the phone book,
And hire a really bad conversationalist.
Working class men make me feel like a girl—and it feels good.

Drugs turned my best friend into a really bad conversationalist.
We used to have discussions that fit together so perfectly—
Watching us talk, people said, was like
Watching the Chinese play ping-pong—

You would walk home after a night like that;
You would feel like you understood
The way the trombone informed the paper clip.

Together, we honestly believed
We could build apartments to put our feet into—
Places we could call *shoes*.

Bobby Pins

A friend involved in prison reform
Would make three-view drawings of his pants;
Then he would give the pants he didn't wear
To friends he didn't like.

When he would shop for shampoo,
He would call it *shampooing*.
He inherited bobby pins that matched the bobby pins he already had,
But that was no reason to be ungrateful.

He would go unnoticed playing dead at Natural History museums
Until they shut off the lights and closed the place.
Then he would have you over to his kitchen;
Where he would peel potatoes with a spoon
Because it was safer, rounder, and stupider that way.

His life was like a receptionist waiting in line to talk to a receptionist
At an Indian hotel casino that had the same floor plan as the city jail.

One Another's Toothbrushes

He said that his sister stole his plastic army men,
And mailed them to relatives in Arizona.
But his claims lacked *credibility* because he wrote acid poetry
About technicolor green macaroni and cheese.

He would come home from high school
And I would be getting drunk with his mom,
Even though he and I went to the same high school.

That was the least of his worries.
At night, the people he lived with would hide
One another's toothbrushes from each other.

His little brother would cross the highway,
Climb the tall tree, and shout the phrases he had heard on television.
He would shout things like, *Zero point nine percent financing—*

His father was always alone, reading great long books like,
The Biography of the Guy Who Grew Up Without Lightbulbs.

His father was a foliage snob.
You say to him: *Wow, those trees are beautiful.*
And he says: *That's nothing; you should go to New Hampshire in about a week.*

A Picture Painter I Know

While he's probably my best friend,
He insists on maintaining this corny Renaissance notion of beauty,
This water lilies and frogs notion of beauty.

I like water lilies as much as the next guy.
But the problem with water lilies is this—
There's nothing we can *do* about them.

He's always drawing my attention to wildflowers growing in a meadow
Or something.
When he should know full well
That I'm more likely to appreciate somebody's garage.

He pays such close attention to such tiny things.
And he looks at everything for too damn long.
He can devote entire afternoons to looking at clouds or twigs
Or whatever.
A painter can look at twigs for seventy-five minutes at a stretch
And consider it a day at the office.

A writer is more interested in the word 'twig'
Which is over with in less than a second.

Once, he called my attention to a sky
Which he said was the 'perfect blue'
You could never mix paint, he said, to achieve such a blue.

Of course he had everything backwards:
Mixed paint, I said, would achieve the perfect sky
In that it would never rain on you, or bring on drought.

Last year we cleaned out somebody's garage.
We took home, among other things,
Mid-century motor oil calendars of painted girls.

Down at the frameshop, the worker called the prints "idealistic."
This is what I said to him, and I was right to say it:
"I don't want realism on my walls—
That's what windows are for."

The Free and Open Exchange of Ideas

We don't buy those things that people put in their toilets
That make the water turn blue.
Because those things turn my piss,
And the piss of my friends and family, green.
Maybe I'll get one on St. Patrick's Day.

I'm sorry about the toilet jokes.
On the other hand, we need to stop apologizing for toilet jokes.
People will have thoughts about toilets,
And they should feel free to express them—
That's how the toilet was invented.

But why do the Irish always insist on
Telling you what county they're from?
I met an Irish guy the other day;
We shook hands, and it wasn't long
Before he was telling me what county he was from.

Looking Forward to Back Surgery

His bicycle ride past the statue in the park;
Some sort of problem occurred,
He went over the handlebars; he *enjoyed* a spinal cord injury.
But his job down at the company was so disappointing—
He was actually looking forward to back surgery.

The surgery was just another flavor of *jury duty*.
The time he brought a book about James Madison along to kill time,
But then they briefed everyone with a videotape about Thomas Jefferson.
He spent the afternoon hoping for a misdemeanor.

The defense attorney would try to *curry favor* with the jury
By comparing the courage of his client to that of a popular football star;
He would compare his defendant's actions to
Those of people on television—
In an effort to normalize the situation.

There was only one attractive woman on the jury—
All these *citizens* were trying to hit on her throughout the deliberation.
They were so lonely, those citizens.
Ultimately, the woman was sent home as an alternate.

The defendant admitted
That he found it hard to pray with a straight face;
That he intentionally opened a beer,
Fully expecting to hear his mother answer, *hello.*

Figure Drawings

Photography was *something*, in that it redefined sentimentality.
People could live in the past with greater accuracy.
The way that airplanes made it possible
For people to imagine unidentified flying objects—

There were plenty of flying objects that could not be identified,
But they were never taken seriously,
Until identified flying objects allowed us to imagine them.

Pornography was certainly a weird scene
Before the development of photography—
During the Napoleonic Wars, or whatever,
You would have like Austrian soldiers
Jerking off to figure drawings of fancy ladies—

It's something to think about—
Soldiers horsing around with figure drawings.

The Right Tool for the Job

You will drive downtown in your *motorcar*,
You will hit a pedestrian crossing a street,
At the very moment you are noticing a road sign
With an image of a pedestrian crossing a street.

Posterity will be more fascinated by American road signs
Than it will be by Canadian photography.

Once, you became *so angry* at not locating
A Phillips head screwdriver,
That you set out on a drinking binge.

You need to be aware
That there is a single answer
That works for every possible question.
The answer to every question in nature is this: *It Depends.*

Be Wary

Be wary of uprisings by groups that do calisthenics.

Never go to bed with anyone
Who uses the phrase *soul mate*.

Understand that it's mostly banal people
Who use the word *banal*.

Never encourage children to play the drums;
Make it explicitly understood
That there is enough percussion in this world already.
Help them establish a Museum of Silence and Industry.

And if they have an opportunity
To buy stolen doll house furniture—
Tell them they may buy the furniture at their own risk.
But if and when the cops show up at their door,
Flush all that doll house furniture down the toilet—

Plumbers can come by later,
To break down the pipes,
And pull those little chairs out.

Old World Craftsmanship

When old guys walk around and whistle,
They're never whistling any particular song—
It's more like a series of random notes.
In the Twenties and Thirties my grandfather probably stumbled upon
Half a dozen Beatles songs
And didn't think anything of them, didn't think they were that good,
Didn't feel like showing them to anybody.
And you know if he didn't, somebody else did.

Some 5 foot 6 inch asshole
Stole my Gibson Florentine mandolin.
Do you know what one of those things is worth?
You could buy a house with one of those things.
They only made about a thousand of them,
And two-thirds of them were sat on.

I'm not saying all the good songs have been written.
But all the good songs have been written.
And most of the bad songs have been written.
I was born at a time when all the obvious ideas had been used up.
It was easy to write the great American novel,
Back when there were only five American novels.
Or that Pythagoras guy with his A squared plus B squared equals, duh—
If I could just go back there and draw parallelograms to a vanishing point,
And dazzle people with arches.
Arches just aren't that impressive—
They're not really that strong,
They don't keep getting stronger as more weight is put upon them.
You can have arches; you can have classical music—
It's European; it's foreign.
I don't like Europe; that's why my family moved here;
They hated classical music.
They hated old world craftsmanship.

They used to call it European craftsmanship
Until they found out England wasn't in Europe.

My little brother used to think that Bebop was played by bees,
Which is really stupid because bees would be really shitty trumpet players
Because their lips are all small, and have all those dumb parts.

Coleslaw

It was one of those hot as hell days—
The sweaters in my closet looked like cruel torture devices.
But fashion is all screwy now anyway;
The hipsters on my block dress like Jehovah's Witnesses.

The Prune Association of America, or whatever, has decided
That prunes should now and forever be called 'dried plums'.
The idea, I'm guessing, is to avoid connotations of elderly bowel imagery.
Poetry, I'm saying, is not insignificant—people are highly paid to
Anticipate our associations with elderly bowel imagery.

They are doing this so that young people who wear
Sneakers that look like big marshmallows
Might hesitate less in the face of prunes,
I think.

My great-great-grandfather probably wore stupid shoes as well,
I don't know—
But when the telephone came out he got so lathered up about it
That he owned two telephones from two different companies
Even though he lived in a one room shack and
Wiped his asshole with the Sears Roebuck Catalogue.

I often feel this misplaced compassion for things.
I feel sorry for coleslaw that goes uneaten.
I told the psychiatrist, I said,
Doc, I anthropomorphize coleslaw—
Never let your kids go down that road.
Mamas don't let your babies anthropomorphize coleslaw.

Someone asked me the other day
If I would like to hold their baby.
I said,
Frankly, I'd rather hold an adult.

Practically a Wash

It's in the newspaper one day, some story.
You notice the principle of supply and demand going on—
It reminds you that you forgot to call your dad.

The television and the pizza box
Make you feel like a third wheel.
You wonder if they cut corners when they built the pyramids.

Nobody goes to the lumberyards anymore except the lumberyard guys;
You take away the lumberyard guys and it's practically a wash.

You notice that the leftists next door
Raise their children with the same
Laissez-faire approach that Republicans use to regulate big business.
Is the cesspool half empty or half full?

Emphysema

I was smart enough as a boy to fashion my own stupidity;
I fashioned the idea that emphysema was the inability to emphasize things.
I imagined that a banjo sounded like a well-organized box of marbles.

Now and then I might say, "Me and my brother,"
And then some adult would correct me, and say, "My brother and I."
But sometimes it would be an adult who *supported the Vietnam War.*
Somehow, the Vietnam War was more *acceptable* than "Me and my brother."

Nobody ever talks about *ladybugs piled up like cordwood;*
But there they were anyway, in my windowsill, at the end of the summer.

Some people look silly wearing hats;
Some people look silly writing poetry.

It's not about choices—
It's about looking or not looking silly.

If that isn't free will, it'll have to do,
Until the real thing comes along.

Comparative Literature

I always saw religious fanatics
As overzealous literary critics, devoid of humor,
Composing stubborn book reports—
Always about the same book, over and over again—
Insisting on the same old interpretation
Of the same old text.

Often they would pass these interpretations on to their children;
Sometimes they would even fire ammunition and throw bombs
At other critics who saw the book differently.

I had to ask myself,
Where does one's body stop and one's T-shirt begin?

Nevertheless, I made up my mind to believe in God,
After looking up "Universe, origin of,"
In an *Information Please Almanac.*

If that isn't Christ, it'll have to do,
Until the real thing comes along.

Far From the Madding Crowd

It was a word that was used once by one man,
Never to be used by anyone ever again,
Except only when referring specifically
To the word's original use,
Or to the man who originally used it.

This poem has done nothing to change that.

I Made Up This Limerick

I bought some dandruff shampoo.
I rubbed it on Albert Camus.
It got in his eye,
He started to cry,
And, Simone de Boo Hoo Hoo.

About the Author

Matt Cook appeared in the five-part PBS series, *The United States of Poetry*, produced by Washington Square Films. His poem 'James Joyce' was aired on National Public Radio's *Fresh Air with Terry Gross*, during a broadcast about spoken word in 1996. He also wrote and performed the original poem, 'Picabo Street', for a nationally televised commercial for Nike during the 1998 Winter Olympics. It was chosen by *Adweek* magazine as one of the Best Creative Spots of February 1998. Cook currently performs *Yesterday's News*, a show of comic monologues on the theme of Milwaukee history, for the Internet television site, zerotv.com. He lives in Milwaukee. This is his first book.

Manic D Press Books

Monster Fashion. Jarret Keene. $13.95
This Too Can Be Yours. Beth Lisick. $13.95
Devil Babe's Big Book of Postcards. Isabel Samaras. $11.95
Harmless Medicine. Justin Chin. $13.95
Depending on the Light. Thea Hillman. $13.95
Escape from Houdini Mountain. Pleasant Gehman. $13.95
Poetry Slam: the competitive art of performance poetry. Gary Glazner, ed. $15
I Married An Earthling. Alvin Orloff. $13.95
Cottonmouth Kisses. Clint Catalyst. $12.95
Fear of A Black Marker. Keith Knight. $11.95
Red Wine Moan. Jeri Cain Rossi. $11.95
Dirty Money and other stories. Ayn Imperato. $11.95
Sorry We're Close. J. Tarin Towers. $11.95
Po Man's Child: a novel. Marci Blackman. $12.95
The Underground Guide to Los Angeles. Pleasant Gehman, ed. $14.95
The Underground Guide to San Francisco. Jennifer Joseph, ed. $14.95
Flashbacks and Premonitions. Jon Longhi. $11.95
The Forgiveness Parade. Jeffrey McDaniel. $11.95
The Sofa Surfing Handbook. Juliette Torrez, ed. $11.95
Abolishing Christianity and other short pieces. Jonathan Swift. $11.95
Growing Up Free In America. Bruce Jackson. $11.95
Devil Babe's Big Book of Fun! Isabel Samaras. $11.95
Dances With Sheep. Keith Knight. $11.95
Monkey Girl. Beth Lisick. $11.95
Bite Hard. Justin Chin. $11.95
Next Stop: Troubletown. Lloyd Dangle. $10.95
The Hashish Man and other stories. Lord Dunsany. $11.95
Forty Ouncer. Kurt Zapata. $11.95
The Unsinkable Bambi Lake. Bambi Lake with Alvin Orloff. $11.95
Hell Soup: the collected writings of Sparrow 13 LaughingWand. $8.95
The Ghastly Ones & Other Fiendish Frolics. Richard Sala. $9.95
King of the Roadkills. Bucky Sinister. $9.95
Alibi School. Jeffrey McDaniel. $11.95
Signs of Life: channel-surfing through '90s culture. Joseph, ed. $12.95
Beyond Definition. Blackman & Healey, eds. $10.95
The Rise and Fall of Third Leg. Jon Longhi. $9.95
Specimen Tank. Buzz Callaway. $10.95
The Verdict Is In. edited by Kathi Georges & Jennifer Joseph. $9.95
The Back of a Spoon. Jack Hirschman. $7
Baroque Outhouse/Decapitated Head of a Dog. Randolph Nae. $7
Graveyard Golf and other stories. Vampyre Mike Kassel. $7.95
Bricks and Anchors. Jon Longhi. $8
Greatest Hits. edited by Jennifer Joseph. $7
Lizards Again. David Jewell. $7
The Future Isn't What It Used To Be. Jennifer Joseph. $7

Please add $4 to all orders for postage and handling.
Manic D Press • Box 410804 • San Francisco CA 94141 USA
info@manicdpress.com   www.manicdpress.com